Striking Water

poems by
paul genega

Grateful acknowledgement is made to the editors of the following publications, in which some of these poems first appeared:

Audit: *The Palazzo Courtyard*; Electrum: *Unlearning How to Swim*; Epoch: *Postcards from Silence*; High Rock Review: *Madame Lucy*; Home Planet News: *Memorial to Labor Day*; The Literary Review: *The Crayfish, Good, A Change of Scenery, Scavenging, Safe Places*; The Nation: *The Courier, Descent and Sentiment, The Rainmaker*; New York Quarterly: *The Self-Made Man*; The Panhandler: *That Summer*; The Reaper: *Aliens*; The Salmon (Ireland): *Brief Encounter, November, Dog, Danse Macabre*; Salthouse: *Mooncusser*; Seattle Review: *Braving It*; Soundings/East: 3: *Kelp, Unlearning How To Swim*; Washington Review: *Long Island Lather, Florida Exotica*; Webster Review: *Walking the Plank*

Typset and designed by The Copy Bureau, Galway, Ireland
Made and printed in Great Britain by
The Guernsey Press Co. Ltd., Guernsey, Channel Islands.

Cover 'The Self Made Man & The Moon' by Aaron Fink,
from 'Perhaps' a portfolio of prints by Aaron Fink with
poems by Paul Genega

ISBN 0948339 21 7 Hardcover £8.50; $12.00
ISBN 0948339 22 5 Softcover £4.50; $7.00

Produced with the financial assistance of Vivien Leone, New York.

Salmon Publishing
Auburn, Upper Fairhill, Galway

for
Jerry Adelmann

Contents

The Crayfish

pinches out of his hard shell
and tingling, all naked,
sways in the cold tank
staring at his former self.

Not just his old clothing,
like the baseball caps
we used to wear, those favorite
plaid jackets, now too tight –

but himself, the corporeal self.
More akin to boy-blonde ringlets
heaped on the barber's floor
but even that's not right.

We'd need our own skins,
the whole flayed hide
tacked above the mantle
to duplicate this crayfish.

And who would want to confront
himself in quite that way;
to face old imperfections;
the unflawed which will spoil;

all which cannot change?
Well, for that matter,
not the crayfish either.
He stares and pokes and prods
and then, he eats it.

Aliens

The night the Martians landed
in Grovers Mills, New Jersey
fear took my father east
all the way to Montauk Point.
Like automatic pilot,
cruise control at ninety –
except his car didn't even
have a Philco on the dash.

I've heard the tale so often
it almost feels like mine.
Careening from doomed Brooklyn
in a black coupe locked like sleep,
past dreams of withered farms,
shingled fishing towns,
scrub oak, sand and pines...
a silent ride, thought frozen,
driven more than driving
till he came to land's end
and the sea slapped him awake.

And there stood Montauk Light
swinging its white blades,
trying to slice the night
into manageable pieces.
And higher up, the stars,
a young man's map of romance,
the fate he'll someday master,
turned suddenly a pox,
each speck untold disaster.

Propped against a bearded rock,
huddled from the wind,
he lit a blue-tipped match,
a little SOS, a minute spark
at the edge of the known world,
and wondered, as men wonder,
as I have wondered too –

What the hell should I do now?
Where in hell do I go now?
Who will come and save me now?

But no one came, of course.
Except for guilt –
in a flash he saw his mother,
my aunts, then gawky kids,
the four of them crouched
in the back bedroom in Bay Ridge.
The airwell window breaking,
a green claw inching closer...
And all he could do
was hold his own damp skin.
All father could do
was hold his own damned skin.

◆ ◆ ◆

It wasn't until dawn,
a rising salt-stained fog,
that hunger took over
and ripped him from that rock.
At a cafe in the village

over homefries and poached eggs,
the waitress informed him
the whole thing was a hoax,
just a Halloween prank.
And she laughed at him,
she laughed, laughed so hard
he thought her eyes
would drop into the plate.

It was 1938 –
in father's words,
the last good year for laughter.
I would not arrive
until a decade later.
But neither of us ever was
the same from that point on.

Kelp

Strange, I wonder most if I'll know
the precise moment you've retrieved
this from the sea. Perhaps I will be
whittling, perhaps eating a pink fish
or hanging more kelp up to dry,
arms full of heavy ribbons, rubber-
tough, brown, when suddenly I'll tingle,
hairs pricking on my neck, and I'll know
you've found the bottle, picked it up,
uncorked it... Strange, I suppose,
to wonder about that now, but life
here works like lungs – sun, moon,
the fifty-eight count shower
each and every afternoon, low tide
(kelp tide) high tide kelp tide;
I know nothing of surprise. How awful
it would be then to spot salvation
someday bobbing the far-line,
me knee-deep in water, unprepared
with proper greetings, merely doing
what is needed to keep generally alive.
Always more kelp to be harvested –
for food, fuel, roof repair, shoes –
about kelp, I now know tons –
which kind makes good eating, which
is best to burn, how to find the giants
even if you cannot swim. How nice
it will be someday to chat with you
about this, seated by a fire, hot drinks
in our hands, feet up and cat purring,

a nice long relaxed chat, or better yet
a listening; it's been ages since
I've listened. I am growing so one-sided.

◆ ◆ ◆

Ha! I made a joke because clearly
this has two sides and I've moved
onto the back. Perhaps that wasn't
such a very funny joke. Here
the ocean laughs at anything
so I'm spoiled in a way. Besides,
I suppose, this is not a joking matter.
Lonely. O lonely. Lonely as the tree.
That's a song I composed yesterday.
I've sung lots since I arrived.
Everyday a brand new lyric.
Everyday a little lonelier and
stupider, I fear. I forget things
all the time, like where I left
my hatchet and the texture of red
meat and which batch on the kelp-rack
needs more time in the sun. One thing
is for certain, I don't need more sun.
My arms and legs look crinkled as
dry kelp. My face feels crinkly too.
I probably even smell like kelp,
like a pungent strand of rack kelp
studded with black flies, half-wet kelp,
the rankest, though the tastiest and
Damn! Damn. Damn, I do go on. But
kelp, understand, has been my life

so long. I forget what people
talk about. I'm forgetting
all the time. What the hell
am I to do? Right now, my friend,
the sun is high above the big bush,
the sea is snickering away, and
I'll need much more kelp till you come.

Madame Lucy

Tonight we will be busy.

All day I am reading the newspaper;
how the earthmouth cracked a smile,
how an arm cradled a needle,
how the sea has turned thick sauce.

All day I am staring at black print
till it all becomes a shimmer,
till the page becomes my window,
till I see it is for certain

tonight we will be busy.

◆ ◆ ◆

Tonight I will raise the bamboo shade
at seven, as I always do, at seven,
and already they'll be waiting,
the sloe-eyed, the bent, the young
with dog breath and wet skin,
they will be waiting,

one after another
nodding past me to the back,
sifting like dust
through the glass beads to the back

◆ ◆ ◆

Till at last Madame Lucy
will stretch in her claw chair,

call to me
her scratchy whisper:

> "Enough, Pablo.
> Enough until tomorrow.
> Tell them good stars
> shine till then."

For me it will be time
to lower the bamboo,
bring to her a cup of beer.

> "Come sit by me,
> Pablocito,"

she will say. And so it is
I'll sit, my head

> "just like a kitten"

in her lap.

◆ ◆ ◆

So hot and red and still the small
back room is. We will sit
like plants there, breathing,
till it comes to Madame Lucy
to ask again when I am born,
if I am happy in her employment,
if I am good to my poor mother,
if I yet desire women.
My words, they'll drift like snow

in the ruts of her black dress.
Her eyes upon my neck,
her hands stroking my hair
O soft
stroking my hair

◆ ◆ ◆

"Listen well, boy,"

she will snap.

    "Do you know why they come every night
    to Madame Lucy?   I tell you
    that they come for they suffer much
    bad luck. Because they are overcome
    with troubles, with conditions
    not natural. Because death or lust
    has taken from them loved ones.
    Because they are blinded by the sun.
    Because they can't see in the dark.

    And only Madame Lucy
    can bring them back to Good."

    "Listen well,"

she will say sharp.

    "Tonight a man gave his hand
    to Madame Lucy. Heavy it was,
    with the feel of wet potato.

In the palm I see something
terrible, sliced deep.
I say 'watch the place your feet go.'
We will say for him a novena."

I'll say, yes, a good novena.

"In the eyes of another
I see a strange red glowing,
hot coals on tree-black hills.
I read for her the tea leaves,
send her home with Holy Water."

For her, a good novena.

"In the cards of the third
is the digging of the spades.
For him I do swear solemn
by the saints who slay the demons..."

Three special good novenas.

"Yes, yes,
Madame Lucy and her Pablo,
the healer and her helper,
together, they do good."

◆ ◆ ◆

There will be silence then
between us,
warm and thick between us
but inside the rag is wrung.

11

"I myself have seen
many dark things, Pablo.
Twice Death has come
and sat with Madame Lucy,
shuffled Tarot at her table.
Twice Death has come
with his mouth red as the poppy,
with his words so soft and sweet."

I must cross myself three times,
touch the Jesu's wounds.

Madame Lucy, she will smile,
stroke my hair and smile,
perhaps press a piece
of silver in my palms
because business has been good.

 "And for you, Pablocito,
 I will also say novenas
 to find a good strong woman
 when it is time."

◆ ◆ ◆

It is time,
at last time,
for me to press my lips
into her hands, her hands
which smell so sweet,
honey sweet and mint,
how my mouth will burn red, cold.
But Madame Lucy, she is old.

Already she will be passing
away from me to sleep,
breasts rising up and falling
beneath a web of lace.

◆ ◆ ◆

I must pull me from her side,
glide through the glass curtain,
raise the bamboo shade.

It will be
the hour of streetsweepers,
girls and yellow taxis
slowly cruising home.
The last star will yet be unaware
that morning has begun.

Of sleep, I can have none.
Feet up on the sill,
I must study the front window
and quietly
work

my song
for Madame Lucy.
I sing. I sing

◆ ◆ ◆

the man taking stairs too quickly,
tumbling, tumbling down;

the woman in the kitchen,
pink sleeves catching flame;

the man whose lungs
give up.

I sing and I sing
and I sing and I sing

so the next night we'll be busy,
and tomorrow night, busy.
She and I, together, busy,
she and I, forever, busy.

For Madame Lucy
sweet
I sing a song
of many sorrows.
I sing
and I sing
and business,
it stays
good.

Braving It

Down the dank
Stairs he proceeds
With wobbling knees,
Blood and breath
Burning, tongue
Tied to his teeth.

Down into a world
Of hiss and thump
He inches, there
To prove himself
Brave by remaining
Sixty counts.

At the last enormous
Step, the boy breaks
Into sweat, freezes,
Starts the call:
One Mississippi. Two
Mississippi. Three

Fourfiveleventwenty-
Seven Mis sis sip pi.

Spiderwolves crouch
In corners. Legless
Dangers hover near.
Flecks of stone
Like constellations

Glint on the damp walls.

Thirty-two Mississippi.
Thirty-three. Thirty-four.

How he loves this
Place he's come to,
This dark which bumps
And leers, this cellar
Of stars, peppered
Manfully with fear.

Unlearning How To Swim

She had forgotten the tequila
and asked if I'd drive with her
to a nearby shopping center.
We pulled into the back lot
then stopped. It was late.
Only the liquor store was open.
She kept the engine running,
like the rumble-hum of ocean.
I wanted a drink desperately.
Her eyes were blue, wet stones
from a seacave. Dark fronds
strained the sea. She looked
and again looked. Dry lips cracked
a smile. It was only a few seconds.
High lampposts palmed light
which made us younger. We were
wading a rock coastline.
The sun and moon were swimming.
We entered a dim seacave.
She smiled in a way which made me
not her son. I wanted to drink
deeply. Her hands crawled
crab-like up the steering wheel.
Words were sleeping in the back seat.
Father was home waiting. Sister was
in Denver. My life was in Manhattan.
The hollow was fast filling,
waves snapping their white fingers.
She was singing beneath water.
My face skin was stinging.

I was unlearning how to swim.
It was only a few seconds.
A black van's headlights screamed
through the rear window. Eyes
darkened into guilt. She turned
off the car engine. Crabs burrowed
in the mud. Fish streamed
towards the horizon. I bought
the tequila. I mixed Margaritas.
I rimmed glasses with salt.
The next day she went back
and crashed the sea into a wall.

Danse Macabre

So quietly he came, quiet
as a cloud, the kind that
angels used. And sometimes,
gently, he'd brush back
my tousle, stand with fixed
expression like a crucifix
or doll. He didn't know
I was watching, didn't know
I was awake, when O so slowly
he undid the white cord of
his pyjamas, let the trousers
fall. Hands on hips, swaying,
untethered, unbound, around
and around he turned, faster
and faster, until even I was
dizzy and had to shut my eyes.
My dream-man, I'd think
in the morning as he stormed
me with his fists, meted out
just punishment for dreaming
my dream or not being asleep.
It didn't much matter which.
For I knew, even as I knew
not to speak the unspeakable,
that I had seen the unseeable,
my father's art, his heaven,
the hard beauty of a mad god.

Under Pius

for Barbara Melchione

Summer was a fan rotating warm shadows,
Winter we knew by the smell of Scotch plaid scarves;
But frankincense was always, beyond season or weather,
Wafting like a murmur from vestibule to apse.

Ladies in mantillas lit candles in red holders,
Chewing prayers the way that we chewed gum.
The coins they dropped caused earthquakes,
Louder even than the crickets the oldest Sisters used
To make us little angels genuflect as one.

Jesus, of course, was there too, burnished on the altar,
Surrounded by the saints. The Virgin was quite pretty,
A Donna Reed in blue; Saint Joseph seemed nice too.

But the heart of the matter really was in back —
The wood stall where the priest sat,
Sliding right the confessional shutters,
Violet stole and flesh blurred behind translucent glass.

It was like whispering to someone kneeling in the shower,
Certain any moment we'd be scolded or scald.
Blood quickened, face flushed, like the rose in a rose window
Convinced we had committed communism somehow.

And also in the back were the racks
Of 10c pamphlets -- *Dating, Divorce, Alcohol, The Jews...*
An entire pocket library of don't's and do's.
The best was *Padre Pio: Our Capuchin Stigmatic*
Whose holy hands we gaped at every chance we could —

20

Sunset as a promise, pain with imprimatur,
More sheerly terrifying than *The Thing or The Fly* --
Though, auguring ill, couldn't bring ourselves to buy.

Postcards From Silence

Long diseased with silence, our mouths
manage an incomplete recovery.
Words form, but mine come out
backwards, a tangle of kc's and ht's
only transformed by using your face
as a mirror. You, though, omit words,
violate syntax. Before you declared:
"I feeling am My is hurt the."
To fill in the holes, I must pantomime
hunger, spleen and abnegation.
That is what I do, disappearing
under blankets, you raised up in wonder,
writhing like a wounded bird:
"Colder me than cube ice?"

Of course there is a relapse.
Doctors are approached. An historian
informs us the problem is with the culture.
He summons a panel of mystics,
longshoremen, Manichaeans and paupers
to face the erring nation. America,
we find, is no more eloquent
than either you or I. It just repeats
its name, a voice stuck in a barrel,
an echo back from steely hills:
"America merica meri..."

"Deal big!" you reply,
and for once I must agree,
upholding what is sacred is the story

of our lives. But I still can't recall
if I was raised in Maine with a collie
named Zeke or in New York with a nanny.
Our stories have been merging
these long eleven years and both of us
fear the coming rainy season. Our phobia
is mudslides, the elements fusing
a movable grave, a sludge
which will sweep us down into the sea.
"Long too," you admit, departing for
home, teetering the rim of our bluff.
But by now I've had enough.

Thus I am writing you postcards
of places I will visit
someday. The oldest Baptist church
in SE Oklahoma, where hymns are sung
louder than the wind. Purple-rose
Las Vegas, where tumblers whir
and silver clinks into my prayerful hands.
Downtown Central City where I hawk
books door to door, pretending
I work to support you.

"Dearest," I begin on the first
of glossy photos. "Smoke rolls
like tumbleweed on the road I am taking
away from you. You think I cannot
travel, wrapped in a blue robe,
secure in wool-lined slippers
but oh how wrong you are. Even now
I am edging east from the coast,

reading my steps left to right
like print. On the stretch just ahead
sand has been spread, smooth
as pure bond paper, to record
the progress of my leaving.
Alone? Of course I'm lonely.
But with a little rain, Los Angeleans
will drive to see the desert blush.
When they come I'll sell my postcards,
the stock already printed with this
longstanding message: WIHS HERE OYU WERE."

Brief Encounter

Beyond the world's weather,
Beneath a peacock sky –
That's where I spent the day.
In a jungle of wet color,
Low clouds grazing
My pink cheeks so gently
I couldn't help but laugh
The way the fern fronds
Laugh, hot dark and green.

How long I roamed alone
I do not know, nor if
The boy in ibex skins
Was waiting just for me –
Stream of corn hair radiant,
Wet-lipped grin expectant.
Across a lake I danced,
Singing my way to him and
Reached his outstretched hands

Just when you walked in.
You, puckered with hello,
Grumbling about supper.
Well, dear, you'll have to wait.
I've had no time to cook.
Today I was away, so far, far
Far away. You don't believe?
Then look – see how clean
The bottoms of my feet are.

A Change Of Scenery

The seventh week camping
on these slopes, our bones
accustomed to the abrupt change
of mountain weather. My foot
forecasts rain, your palms splay
before the wind kicks up.
There seem few surprises left.

Like the stones and trees
of the scenery, we stay put.
No longer beating through the brush
to view the blue lake, the grove
of skinny birch, that herd
of lazy ruminants. We've
signed this patch of land

with our tent, the khaki tent
we uncomfortably call home
as if home for us
could be pegged into the dirt
without resounding horns (saxophone
or taxi) without the bright
aurora on the Empire State.

Before bed we build a fire,
declaim volcanic fountains
which built this awesome range.
But above dark mounds and heaths
we see no sparks. Only stars
erupt at night, sprays of cold
light, the windows of this world.

Descent And Sentiment

The plane makes its descent on
the city where I lived once, flickering
Interstates, cloverleaves and loops,
as if Omaha, exploded, had strewn
its ruby innards from sea to shining sea.
Still, there is the roc egg of the Capitol,
floodlit – there, Washington's white cock,
things recognizable amid the squat
flat-top office buildings, all built
since I've been gone. I remember D.C.

Southern – waxy magnolias, ornate columned
mansions of mustachioed ambassadors,
unbreathable summers, and you, dreamer,
drifter, odd-jobber, first honest love
in a rowhouse long ago. I remember that
whole summer beneath your sloping roof,
laughing at nothing, drinking too much
wine. We spoke three words through August
then firmly shook good-bye. Me, back
to Nebraska; you to Virginia, I think.

Now, here, buckled to my speeding seat,
I search, despite myself, for our
rowhouse gable, for the window strobed
with candles and moon, though surely razed.
Of course I cannot find it, more than count
these lights, the beds I've known since you.

27

By landing the runway is just a blur
of blue. Then the wheels touch, touch down
firmly, and the dim dishonest longing
for the long gone bursts in flame.

The Rainmaker

He used to rely upon rumor
to find work, farmers and their wives
eager to enumerate the hardships
of others – up north,
the corn was small as carrots;
out west, wheat had burned.
Too often, though, such gossip
proved just a way of gloating
or simply defense of their own
stunted growth and he learned
like any rainmaker to count
only on the sky – swift white wisps
clawed and batted by cat winds,
the lunacy of blue, suns drunk
on themselves and burning
for still more. These signs
now show the way. And before
horizons sizzle, before brown
crumpled plants appear along
the roadside, even before the taste
of dust, he knows what lies ahead.

Perched on the cracked gray planks
of his old wagon, he swirls
into a town, looking every inch
like a man who could work weather –
face deviled with arroyos, saltflats,
ruts, straw hair scoured white.
Hesistant, slow, a crowd
starts moving towards him,

pushed by desperation beyond
bashfulness or doubt -- until
at last their shuffling stops,
long thin fingers knot,
and huge eyes lock in stares.

Used to be he stuttered through
the speech, now he enters it
like sleep, describing his induction
into certain ancient rites,
his anointed role to serve
those cursed with drought.
Up goes a gleaming pitchfork,
thrust high above his head.
But no, my friends, he shouts,
this is not some common farm tool.
Behold the fabled *kaval*, conductor
of elements, wielder of winds.

If they'll just procure some
water, a cup or two of water,
water, something silver, a fistful
of dirt, he will loose its ancient
forces once again. Promises
of cumulus, white clouds clenching
into fists, and rain. Rain!
The ground to break forth
in wondrous abundance, unimaginable
lushness, seas of green... The moon,

only the moon, hears him
jingle away later, watches winds

gouge his face deeper
like the landscapes he seeks.
Back again on the cracked planks
of the wagon, he rides night
like a storm — hears the thumping
wheels as thunder, sees dust clouds
as mist, feels sweat down
the spine like a sudden spring
downpour. Above him, stars,
dreams which have been frozen.
Ahead, more of the same.
The rainmaker looks forward,
makes the lightning rip, moves on.

November

Of the many nightmares I've made,
The worst, I think, watching the cold sea,
Is the one in which I discover myself
Changing, not yet changed, but changing
Into something not-quite human, some-
Thing of the shadow world, where the wild
Romp and randy about with themselves.

In that dream sometimes I have horns,
Not even stuck in appropriate places
Like a nice old myth, but at shoulder blade
Or abdomen, a clump at the top of the hand,
A whorl of calcium on the bottoms of my feet...

What I've done to the body,
What I would do to the body,
What will be done in indefatigable time
Seems so very sad now standing on this bluff,
Sea air softly purring, the waves
Gently licking the green fur of the beach.

Dog

The light, my friend,
I see you standing
in a light so bright
and white it's painful.
In the distance, water
winks like a dizzy
old flirt, but here
on the soft sand
of a dune, you seem
somehow to solidify –
lean-limbed, released,
sniffing the wind of
eternity. And almost
grinning, you hold
that pose, proud,
totally assumed.
Until moved by what –
ever it is moves you,
you sprint down
the slope and run,
run and run. Run,
dark speck making
for the ocean, over
the next crest and
nowhere to be found.

Good

for the film-maker
Bill Daughton (1949-1987)

On the morning of your
dying, you rose camel-
awkward from bed and
took yourself into
the bright white cell
of shower, shrugged
off the hospice gown,
that body-stained rag,
that yellowy chrysalis,
placed it unneatly
on the sanitized floor,
and naked as your first
day on this earth,
with the purple lashes
of dying all over,
skeletal, distended,
you squatted in the tub,
water flaring from
the fixture in a steady
rush of roaring for one
whole luxuriant hour,
lifting eyes once only
from the warm and wet
to whisper, this feels
good, love – love
this feels so

Mourning

I pick up the
telephone, place
the receiver to
my ear, but there
is no number
to dial. The ma-
chine gives a
high hum. Sixteen
seconds it lulls
me with its hum
until a series
of clicks inter-
rupts, as if some
system were trying
to kick in, as if
someone some-
where were trying
to get through.
Then the bleats
begin – loud –
staccato – ur-
gent, but they
too stop at last.
And there's no-
thing but static,
drone general
as snow, like
the nightly news
in purgatory,
an electric sea
in a black shell.

Safe Places

Corners, for example. Corners
Of kitchens, in particular.
Or closets, behind the line
Of overcoats and jackets
Wrapped in cleaner's plastic.
In bed, quilt up to the neck.
Better even – under. Wherever
Doors are locked, double-locked,
Bolted. Windows barred. Drapes
Drawn. Walls covered with cork.
All the mirrors shrouded
With starched white sheets.

Florida Exotica

for Adam Hammer

Hot Christmas! I thought,
What a time to visit
Florida, where the girls are
Decked out in their citrus
Groves tending to the lemons
And key limes of my mind.

I came first to the panhandle,
Crossed the well-marked border
When the baking day was done.
Flamingos folded in themselves,
Pink and brittle as the sunset
Over cypress. O I wanted to go

Slow. But the moss whispered
Me-am-me and south I knew
Were mermaids and alphabetized
Flowers and birds which eat
With spoons. O Sunshine State!
I cried aloud. O Florida exotica!

I drove holding a dream
Through the state
Shaped like a boomerang –
Fast on a road
Slicing the gnarled dark
Where Brooklyn can come back at you.

Long Island Lather

When the blackback gulls
took the beach to feed
and wind turned water white,
we repacked the wicker basket,
folded our green blanket
and drove the five miles home.
Hungry, sunburned, thirsty,

beat, I could feel
the seagrit scratching
in the crotch of my damp suit,
my sister squirming also
on the burning plastic seat.
How I wanted to be home
instantly and hoped we would

never get there. God would
we never get there – where
to save time and hot water
(the boiler was pre-war)
we paired up for the showers.
Sister and mom on the first floor,
father and I way upstairs.

Never since so naked
as with him in that tub.
His hands fidgeting
with the faucet, proffering
white soap. Frothy lather
streaked and spread through
black hair everywhere –

my father's – everywhere.
In that loud warm world of water
we lingered, he and I,
sand streaming off our bodies,
gathering at the drain –
me the whole time less a boy
than the inside of a clam.

Till suddenly – it was over.
The thick mystery of steam parted
and lifted. In its stead,
a pinching chill. Quickly
we'd towel off, slap on powder,
dress for dinner, coming redfaced
and stiff to the set table.

Memorial To Labor Day

I remember best the hours
after supper, watching the sea
violet, the thin summer sunlight
deepen, disappear. I remember the rhythm
of the porch swing which held father,
the roiling chowder pot that mother

scoured and re-scoured. Poor mother,
she seemed to spend all her hours
in the kitchen that summer. Neither father's
reprimands nor the cajoling of the sea
could dissuade her fierce rhythm
of more work and more. Daylight

gone, she retired. First light
of morning, back poor mother
was, battling the rhythm
of summer with her broom. One hour
alone she allowed herself sea-
side, muddling the tide pools. Father,

in all fairness, father
would beg her, relax, lighten
up, please, we're on vacation. But mother
couldn't care less. One hour with the sea
was enough, she'd snap back. And the hours
cooking, cleaning... Well, the rhythm

of life doesn't stop in Amagansett; the rhythm
of work never stops. Anywhere. Sometimes father

tried shaming her to rest, making light
of all her labors. Then for hours
she'd harangue him on mother-
hood and marriage, the stupid wastrel sea.

Only once, as I recall, did the sea's
stock rise in mother's eyes. The wild rhythm
of a nor'easter was raging and mother
eased into a kind of calm. Father
looked nervous all those cold dark hours,
the bruised sky suffused with greenish light

but she for hours watched the stormlight knotting,
breathing in its rhythms. I remember father saying
the sea, she's like a mother. I remember her laugh.

Late August

Rented house – an egg crate of small bedrooms.
The welcome smell of mildew as if time were a tom.

Each day you lugged a jug with a spigot
to the beach, swam in sweet iced tea,
listened to the murmur of Red Barber baseball.

Ah yes, the grin and bear it of board games
when it rained. But mainly it was light,
white beaten with yellow, the sun setting
ineluctably early, the sea warmer than air.

Nights, everyone had ice cream or drove
golf balls into whale mouths. Later,

on the bottom bunk, you'd think of lips you'd kiss
if life were like the movies, up and down
the back roads, dragging a mustang to death.

That Summer

That summer we stacked notions
On the cobweb shelves of Levin's Five & Dime.
Nights, returned from love in the last row
Of the loge, we walked the pine grove
Father had planted when he first married

Our home. With each hard step we took
Rustling the brush, a dove whooshed
From the treetops – the sky flushed into
Frenzy until the dark wings beating
Terrified us inside, naked on our beds.

All that summer the sky appeared
Crooked, untrustworthy,
Like a friend caught in a lie.
Once, as if a habit reprimanded daily
Had been performed one too many times

The air assumed a mean-spirited silence
Then loosed paeans of rage –
Clouds dropping
To the townhall tower clock,
Sending hands flying, battering its face...

Later, sky ascended to a high
Whistle of blue, everywhere there were
Butterflies, kissed to life
By some breathtaking enchantress,
Borne by a wind we both wanted to own.

And that summer also grandmother lay dying
On a leased hospital bed. If nobody was
Looking, we would crank her up to sitting
And proffer a craved cookie, delighting
As she snatched it like a shy, wild bird.

Already more avine than human that summer,
She sometimes attracted others
Of her kind – starlings by the hundreds
Descending on the driveway, the pinetum,
The garden, the lawn chairs, the door...

But the old woman did not fly
That summer while we stayed
Vaguely ill – humorless
And dizzy, ravaged by itches
We could not seem to quell.

Flushed one night with fever,
Stumbling past curfew, we first
Discovered even home could change –
In mother's greenhouse, a cereus had exploded,
Its heavy mauve odor coating every room.

Drunk on a beer and the mere thought
Of that flower, bent on reaching
An intoxicated pitch, we snuck
Our first sweet brandies and waited
For sunrise to watch the flowers die.

They did not die, however. Just as nothing
That summer worked the way we'd thought.

Wax lips, those blooms lasted for weeks.
Their sex and death smell lingering –
In the pines, in the loge, at Levin's,

In our beds – lingering like that summer
When anything could happen, that summer
When everything and nothing seems to happen,
That summer which lingers, lingers and lingers,
Like the long adolescence of American men.

Scavenging

There is always room for more
in the cart I tow
along the back of industry.
Iron, oilcloth, various acetates,
the good pulley string snapped,
the faithful lever
grease can't restore to service –
these things I pile high
without expectation.

I do not recycle, sculpt or sell.
Washers which do not fit
any extant screw
are nothing more to me
than cut metal. I claim
no sentiment for this stuff.
No analogies. No symbols.
I collect because ...
I collect; yes, I collect.

The played-out, abandoned and worn
have a simple fascination.
And it's precisely because
my load lacks value,
lacks utility or purpose
that a pleasure is extended.
Rust, after all,
is a special sort of gilt.
Time provides patina.
Jagged edges worn smooth
are easier to hold.

All right, I confess it,
I find these objects – pretty.
But knee-deep in goldenrod,
paralleling train tracks,
I cannot consider
how loss relates to beauty,
how production must make waste.

I keep busy at my task
without hope of advantage
to myself or to others.
Mine is a happy burden,
a frivolous work
and work is what I do.

Tugging a full cart, I travel
between cities, circumventing
contact with people when I can.
Oh of course when I was younger
the longwinded names titillated some –
Tuscaloosa, Tallahassee, Boca Raton –
even now such names
can muster up what's missing.

Once near Chattanooga
a boy flapped his fingers at me
from a fast west-bound train.
I was rich that day in plastics,
a variety of rare scraps
thus much under strain.
Even more since the sun
was pounding my bare back.

It wasn't out of malice
but I spurned the silly waving.
Speak now of Tennessee
and that excited fat hand,
the sun's hot red fist,
will jab at my side.
I'll think plastics –
Lovely plastics!

But understand this:
if my effort has intent
it is the opposite of recall;
it is, to be exact,
a putting of things behind.

Mooncusser

for Jim Werkowski

Mooncussing: luring ships with bonfires or lanterns onto rocks and shoals for plunder.

1.

I breathe bayberry
till midnight –
the air so thick with it,
I think, the moon alone
could exude such aroma.

She is a full bloom
this night –
three schooners
are sailing her light
east of Madequecham.

Squat on the chill beach,
I watch them disappearing,
fluttering off like moths.

The further they fly,
smaller, the more I feel
the chase – feet scuttling,
working sand to water

until I tumble under.
All night I dream the moon,
awake glowing in my own sweat.

Today, I go to town
for apples and lamp oil.

2.

At the Jethro Coffin House
I learn The Providence
went down
a league off Eel Point.

The talk is buoys and jetties.

When the moon fails her purpose
these waters can turn treacherous.
Shoals and rocks. Crazy rip tides.

I just happen to recall
The Orb was smashed
to drift the size of thumbnails
on Tuckernuck Bar
and only three months later
The Hope and Susan faltered
near Coatue Beach.

What remained of those wrecks?
someone asks – a shard or two
of china? tin of old beef jerky?

From the window of the inn
I see women veiled black,
walking cobblestones
for flour and for prayer.

3.

Like those who go to sea
I will not learn to swim
but today I take the waters
at Tom Nevers Head.

One must enter
these things
slowly –

feet must numb,
calves must numb,
thighs must numb
and upwards...

before taking the plunge
to divest oneself of face salt,
pore produced or eye.

I note this as occurring –
things which shrink
or curl in icy water
resume their normal posture
once returned to land.

4.

*Notes Towards a Theory of Natural
Predaciousness, Being a Series of
Firsthand Observations of Beasts
Terrestrial, Marine and Aerial –*

Sheep and dulse.
Green urchins and coraline weeds.
Jonah crabs and waved whelks.
Ribbon worms and bristle worms.
Common terns and sand launce.
Anemones and hermit crabs.
Serpent stars and quahogs.
Channeled whelks and barnacles.
Laughing gulls and sea skates.
Slipper snails and diatoms.
Clipper rails and fiddlers.
Sanderlings and mole crabs.
Nereis and ghost shrimp.
Night scud and the moon.

5.
I find the moon tonight
lolling in the mudflats,
wading slowly
towards the rocks
at Tom Nevers Head.

No holdfast
is strong enough
to keep her. She slips
in and out of eel grass,

glides through
knotted wrack and kelp,
sowing as she passes
barnacle and periwinkle,
limpet constellations.

Insidious live thing,
the moon —

sea farmer,
dream thief,
snail mother,
creeper,

whore of her
own pleasure,
absconder of
bright treasure,

fat
white
on the mudflats...

6.

Scheduled today, The Lady Jane
back from Cyprus and Marseilles.
Silk, silver, oranges and opals,
an array of the finest
from France and The Levant.

First I buy a fork,
a soup bowl painted
with stars and flying eagles.

Then without
much else to do...

I board the ship
anchored in the harbor,
drape a scarf of fog
across my face,
clang pewter spoons together
and dervish on deck

to the claps and whistles
of an admiring crew.

One sturdy lad,
all legs and smiles,
plays a squeeze-box
as I sing
and O
but it is lovely...

till I feel her
eyes upon me,
feel her
spying on me...

till I see the moon
has dreamed herself
into the noon sky.

7.

The moon is rank tonight
rotting on the compost heap.
I placed her there
with the primrose hedge
and beach plum

which had eclipsed my vision
of waves which come to bow.

Now I watch the moon
like a mushroom cap discolor,
tetter into brown.

Already I have dug
a wide and shallow trench
to bury her once she's been
pulverized to powder.
In two weeks, I'll have mulch.

Then in black fields
sharp stars will sprout
to tangle staunch ships.

I sit deep in thought
this dank night.
Such queer feelings
orbit as I write.

8.

They feel so close
this evening,
close as the candle
swooning on the table,
all those I have known –

a mother who hummed
as she shook out the sheets,
who demanded shoes removed

on entering her home,
who knew how to cool a forehead;

a father,
tall,
with mysterious hands;

two brothers
who laughed at my haircuts,
who run still
through hot quick sunlit dreams;

a supple body
stretched out in elm shade,
tufts of spring grass
and birdsong all around.

I call to them and
call to them, call
to them and call...

Rap once, I just tell them.
If you hear me, just rap once.
Rap once if you are there.

Rap once – rap once –
if you hear me, just rap once –

9.

All those hours squandered
studying her brow, the imagined
intent in the twist of her lips.

All those many nights,
as others will tonight,
I have lifted eyes believing,
believing the moon
would gaze back in my eyes.

But no, I now discover
that's not a pasty face
glooming down upon me
but the bald head of a hag –
bumps and dents, bulging veins
on a scarred hairless crown.

The only hope is science
if the moon's to be outwitted.
Those swells and dips,
ridges and hollows,
will show her true proclivities,
her absolute true Nature.

It would take her very twin
to comprehend her wholly...

But me,
I keep
a wild head
of hair
and plot her
slow demise,
one tiny
nude bump
at a time.

10.

Tonight,
tonight it happens
on Tuckernuck Shoal.
Clouds force the moon
into retreat and
dark winds take the beach.

Walking on water,
dressed in winter white,
I raise a lamp of welcome
to my boys
and send my song out,
out beyond the breakers —

>*Come,*
>*My angels,*
>*Come.*
>*Closer now,*
>*Approach,*
>*Into these shallows,*
>*Jagged jaws,*
>*These narrows.*
>*Feel these*
>*Sharp teeth.*
>
>*I am*
>*The father*
>*Lighthouse*
>*That you seek.*

I am
Your island
Mother
In the kitchen,

Smell my fresh pies,
My nicely warm biscuits
Smeared with plum preserves.

I am
The girl
Who has been sitting
By the fire,
Knees damply
pressed together
Since you left,
Since you hovered
The horizon.

Come closer.
Yes, come
Closer.
Come. Home,
You're almost
Home.

And then yes how they come,
on darting wings back
from Celebes, Annam,
from fabled topaz shores,
their ship returns...

The firm bow impales itself
on rock, begins
its awesome writhing
as I watch. Waves
break and waves break
and break. Waves and O
the rush of it and roar –

I go to pieces.

11.

And all of these are mine.
Someday it will be known
that these and more are mine –

Improvement, sank off Eel Point.
Progress, down at Squam Head, same year;
at Coatue – The Rising Star,
Fair Play, Hope and Susan;
at Tuckernuck – The Orb,

The Shooting Star, two years later;
now the frigate Century
has been taken.

I am weary and spent
from my work.
But in furious days
as men made
their mark on history,
let it be known
I abrogated nothing –

I too have prospered through
enterprise and commerce.

12.

I find one on the beach,
face in the sand,
hands white as the sand.

Though heavy in my arms,
I hold him,
gently rock him,
softly sing a lullaby
that might have given pleasure.

But when I turn him over
for one morsel of wet lips
O how that face shocks.
Bloated and pale, it is
the awful, inescapable,
mocking head of... her.

I drop the thing at once
into a wide and shallow trench,
vow from now on to desist.

And yet but
I'll have treasure.
First, a piece of treasure.
For patience, for invention,

to ease my pain, a treasure.

One last time, a treasure,
a treasure, yes, a treasure...

And I snip
a shiny button
off his black and tattered coat.

The Self-Made Man

*An uneducated former barber, 49, living
in poverty since he was horribly dis-
figured when he fell down a flight of
stairs, has stupefied the Brazilian
medical world by carrying out fifteen
plastic surgery operations on himself.*
                    NEWSDAY 5/22/77

Children called me Werewolf,
said I entered Barra Mansa
every Friday midnight, ravenous
for flesh. It was true I traveled
rarely into town, but when I ran out
of salt or fruit to make preserves
I was forced to take the risk.
Old women, fat in black cotton,
crossed themselves whenever I passed.
Others threw stones. And I was quick
to learn the fear of bad dreams
walking. One night, I caught
an image of myself, dripping
raw meat from a cavernous mouth-hole,
letting blood saliva slide
down the eight horned bumps
which once had been my chin.
I heard me howling at the moon,
heard me begging her to hurl
herself on me, on Barra Mansa.

The moon, she would not listen
to the fever in my wolf-prayer

but rose with her old jokes
told in horrible white-face.
"How," she cracked and cackled,
"is ebb tide akin to a lonely
man's morning?" "At what time of day
will lovers take white-lightning?"
Spiders and ringtails laughed
in the trees, mocked me and sneered
till I lurched at the sky,
spit heavy on my tongue, and screeched
my name with curses. It was then —
precisely then — claws shredding
the low Southern Cross, I came to
clearly see the moon, a face squashed,
misshapen and pockmarked as my own.
Thus like the moon I could alter
what I showed, cut away my face
and rebuild what had been lost.

Authorities call me the self-made man,
a kind of modern miracle.
Over and again I have told them
how I started by shaving off chest hairs,
flaying strips of skin, slowly
reconstructing my left cheek and ear.
I have had to repeat how I melted
plastic whistles and shaped myself
a nose, how I fashioned a full-lipped
new mouth. The instruments I used
through the long months of labor
have been taken to the city
where they are currently displayed

at a medical museum. I remain
a poor man and hope the razor
or scissors will soon be returned
so I might ply my trade as barber.
Since the officials came from Rio,
every beard wants trimming
by the Barra Mansa Werewolf.

The doctors and the villagers
who tortured me a year ago come and
count my ears, marvel at my forehead,
ask me how I did what I simply
had to do. I answer, I was desperate.
I never tell them of the moon,
my sad disfigured lady, but she knows
what is true. Now when she is fullest
I aim my thoughts upward and
suggest how she might change –
tighten up her jowls, make her eyes
symmetrical. She does not listen,
the moon, she never listens,
and reappears the next month
in all her bright non-beauty.
I grow tired of my talking and lie down
outdoors beside her, that hideous head
gently rolling on my shoulders. Then
as sleep begins to take, I show the moon
my love, the way I show my scars.

The Palazzo Courtyard

below is made of special
yellow brick. Notice how carefully
each row has been lain,
how smoothly and precisely
each unit fits the next.
Even here from this high
balcony, we can see
the bond is unique. It was

employed by the master
mason Caratouchi
in the mid-quattrocento
for a mere twenty years
then abandoned
as too time consuming and costly
for practical purposes.
When the Levant trade

collapsed, halting supplies
of Anatolian clay
needed for the veneer,
these building methods ceased.
The Caratouchians,
however, survived longer, until
their last scion Gabriele
squandered what remained

of the family fortune
and let exacting standards
go to seed. The last

structure completed under
    that once-proud family name
was the Palazzo Sparata
    five and a half kilometers
from here. Should you visit

    the estate, I urge you
to observe how craftsmanship
    declined, how the mortar humps up
in the joints, how the simple
    alternation of headers and
stretchers seems closer
    to the Flemish, how the bricks
are chipped and loose,

    worn in the middle,
how far it is afield from
    the virtuoso brickwork
you see here. Consider these bricks
    which lie flush, the thin blue
mortar forming miraculous swirls
    without intruding
on the symmetry. Consider how

    each brick has remained
in its place. It was the decree
    of the Caratouchians –
until Gabriele –
    that none of their constructions
know the weight of man,
    the press of feet or hands.
Since the last worker patched

the last corner, no one
has stepped in this yard.
Nearly six hundred years
and not a hint of the destruction
from use, the destruction
inherent in use.
Observe here what man
builds without man in mind.

The Kings Of The Balkans

The kings of the Balkans
Sit in their Great Hall,
Gilt flaking from the walls
Like an incurable sunburn.

Some still sport their
Crowns, sapphires plucked
By the rank crows of the age.
Most though wear only

Their own black matted hair,
Mutter in a language
Unintelligible to others.
Their common tongue is hunger.

See how they speak
As the shuffling servant
Wheels the serving cart.
Hands storm blackened bread,

Piling pieces by the plates,
Filching from the weakest.
Soon the Keeper of the Butter
Will arrive. The kings will slather

Toast, break out a fresh
Deck - all evening to gamble
And grumble, as the charred towers
Rise again and crumble.

Walking The Plank

This short road ends
in air. No, I do not
want to take it, but
the law of this ship
worried by winds
only witches bring
says I must, and if
I must, allow me
this – to walk
the path of wood
with both eyes open.
Tie the red kerchief
around your own
thick neck, or –
coward, blind yourself.
Me, I want to see
the exact edge,
the thin shaved end
of my existence,
walk towards it
back straight
as the pine plank,
all the ticking
thumping things
still working,
taking in – what?
a splinter? one whiff
of far off earth?
the miffed cries
of the petrels?

cold salt?
I want to gaze
back at the sun,
the hard father
of the day.
I want to catch
the moon adrift
in drowsy blue,
to see these feet
too big still
for the rest of me
at their final
solid moment,
to meet the ocean
eyeball to eyeball
and feel her
long white lashes
slowly close.

The Courier

for Jan Karski,
the Polish courier sent by
the leaders of the Warsaw Ghetto
to inform the world of the Holocaust

I am carrying the sea
in my cupped hands.
Not drops of it, not liters,
the whole dark sloshing sea.
Claws pinch. Nettles sting.
Teeth rip at my palm lines.
It hurts to hold this much,
to be so small and human,
running, running,
as the bloody sun runs –
west – carrying the sea
in my cupped hands.
The faster my legs move,
the more I try to get there,
the more I fear I spill.
Rancid fish and wrackweed,
broken shell and coral,
mark my travel like a tideline.
Everywhere I've been
I have sown salt.
Everywhere now, the rich
green earth laid waste.
But I do not look behind,
not behind and not above,
where the white moon
nightly is devouring

the stars, first in nibbles,
then vast mouthfuls,
bloating like a leech,
whipping storms
as cruel as history
inside my pressed hands,
these poor dumb beasts,
my hands. How much they want
to toss it all away,
to empty it in trenches,
to wall it up for good.
How much I want to fold
myself in pine boughs,
to lie on high ground
humming, to be free
of this thing I've been
anointed with, so
horribly, to make it all
mad fancy, mere nightmare.
It is not. Straight ahead,
face forward, I must run,
run, as the bloody sun runs –
west – and bring the sea
for the whole wide world
to hold. The journey is
a minute. A millennium. Both.
But I do get there. I do.
I am ushered to a chamber
of telephones and chairs,
an ordinary room
of the twentieth century.
Three well-dressed men

walk in, mopping brows
with well-starched hand-
kerchiefs. I want to beg
forgiveness, to explain
I'm just the courier,
a small man, insignificant,
that the news is not
the messenger. But my words
are lost in wind. The three
stand stiffly, staring.
They smile. They nod.
And I... I let it go,
waves of salt and bone
flooding from my hands,
drowning all the ordinary
rooms of this century.
And the next. From the sea
floor I start rising through
a maelstrom black as ink,
past the dead eyes of the living,
the live eyes of the dead...
till I surface with my hands,
two smooth and separate shells,
knifed open like an oyster
which can never join again.